Job
Call Centre
Worker

Royston Butterscotch

For Ali x

John the Call Centre Worker

Royston Butterscotch

This is John. He works in a call centre.

A call centre is a big place where lots of people work.

In a call centre, most people sit at their desks and answer telephone calls all day long.

This is what John does. He answers telephone calls all day long.

He is an important member of staff.

A very important member of staff.

6am!!

One sunny Monday morning, John was at work.

His shift started at 6am, long before many of the other people in Happytown were awake.

You didn't think that people started work that early did you?

Well, it's true! They do!

Some people do start work at 6am.

Have you ever seen 6am?

That morning, John had a phone call from a Mr Williams.

Mr Williams was unhappy with the service that John's company had provided. This made Mr Williams unhappy and grumpy.

John sighed. He had phone calls like this all day long.

You also didn't know that people phoned other people to complain at 6.15 in the morning did you?

Well, it's true! They do!

- Coffee
- TEA
- CHOCOLATE
- DISH WATER

John tried as best as he could to help Mr Williams. But grumpy Mr Williams was still not happy.

John told Mr Williams that he was going to speak to his supervisor.

He put grumpy Mr Williams on hold while he went to the vending machine to get himself a coffee. He needed one.

When he got back to his desk, grumpy Mr Williams was still on the end of the phone. John was kind of hoping that Mr Williams would have hung up.

But no, he was still there.

Mr Williams was still unhappy. He demanded to speak to the manager.

But John's manager was on holiday in Barbados again.

John decided to make an executive decision.

That's right – with his big fat finger, he cut grumpy Mr Williams off - just like that!

No more grumpy Mr Williams.

John thought that the chances of getting Mr Williams back on the phone must have been a million to one. He'd pulled off a brilliant trick.

None of his managers would notice because they were either at home in bed or on holiday in Barbados.

This made John very relieved.

But guess what?

That's right! John got Mr Williams on the very next call that he answered.

John sighed another big sigh.

There was no way he would be able to cut him off again.

John wished he'd never got out of bed.

etc

Grumpy Mr Williams asked for John's name so that he could report him for cutting him off.

John told him that it was John.

Mr Williams asked for John's surname. But John told Mr Williams that he didn't have to provide a surname.

Mr Williams got very angry indeed.

He got so angry that he said a very naughty word.

John told Mr Williams that he shouldn't swear. But this made Mr Williams more angry and he said even more naughty words but this time louder.

John stood up at his desk in case he wanted to lash out at his monitor with his fists.

Mr Williams carried on swearing and shouting on the end of the phone. John reminded Mr Williams that the call was being recorded for training and security purposes. But that didn't stop Mr Williams. He was going mental down the phone.

John could hear Mr Williams smashing up his house and punching himself in the face.

After a few minutes, Mr Williams got bored and calmed down.

etc

John asked Mr Williams if he had calmed down but that started Mr Williams off all over again.

This time, John could hear Mr Williams strangling his cat and throwing his big telly around the room.

John put Mr Williams on loudspeaker so that all the other people who were working at 6.15am could hear.

They laughed and they laughed and they laughed.

It took Mr Williams a good ten minutes to calm down again.

By now, John was getting unhappy himself. He knew the girl he fancied on the other desk had just got up for a fag break.

Yes - at 6.15 in the morning! Can you believe it?

John wanted to go for a fag break himself so that he could chat her up and perv over her tight blouse.

But Mr Williams didn't want to go. He wanted the problem resolved there and then. So he made John stay on the phone and talk.

But just then, John had another plan. A plan that would make him feel happy again.

John asked Mr Williams if he knew who he was talking to.

"John." said grumpy Mr Williams.

"But do you know my surname?" asked John.

"No." said Mr Williams.

etc

"Good," said John, "Then FUCK OFF!" he shouted at the top of his voice.

And with that, he cut Mr Williams off again with his big fat finger.

Then John went to the nearest vending machine and kicked the shit out of it.

About the Author

Royston Butterscotch is a world-renowned, award-winning and very handsome author.

Published by Honey Farm Books

**More jobs stories available at
www.honeyfarmbooks.com**

Printed in Great Britain
by Amazon